RUSTINGTON
A Pictorial History

RUSTINGTON
A Pictorial History

Mary Taylor

Phillimore

1998
Reprinted 2009

Published by
PHILLIMORE & CO. LTD.
Madam Green Farm (Business Centre), Chichester,
West Sussex, PO20 2DD

www.phillimore.co.uk

ISBN 978-1-86077-615-1

Printed and bound in Great Britain

*I would like to dedicate this book to my husband Bev,
our two sons, Andrew and Graeme and their families, with my love.*

List of Illustrations

Frontispiece: Rustington Mill

Acknowledgements

I would like to thank Beckett Newspapers, for permission to use the Neville Duke photograph no. 60, and also Middleton Press, for permission to use 'The Hoover Express' photograph, no. 25. Photographs nos. 81 and 82 are by kind permission of the United States Archives, Washington. I am also grateful to Mr. and Mrs. J.H. Manning, late of Smuggler's Nursery, for their interest, as well as the valuable information about nurseries in the village and the glass-house crops. I wish also to thank Tony Chapman for passing on information about Rustington which he has found while researching local newspapers.

My thanks are also due to Graeme, my son, for all the help he has given me. However, most of the credit for this book must be given to my husband, Bev. Apart from his help with the research, he has spent long hours coming to terms with his computer, as well as endeavouring to transcribe my hand-written scripts in time for publication. His patience and encouragement have always been there when I have needed them — Thank you, Bev.

Introduction

Early History

Rustington, a village set between the South Downs and the sea, seems to have been inhabited from very early times, judging by the many archaeological artifacts that are constantly being found within its boundaries. The fertile soil of this coastal plain, with the forests to the north and the sea to the south, made Rustington a very attractive and safe place to live. There was also plenty of water from the springs, the tidal Black Ditch and an ample supply of salt.

In 1986, the author and her husband were called in to inspect one small area of a perimeter trench (dug to prevent access by travellers) around a field, now the site of Sainsbury's. Their findings prompted them to call in David Rudling and his colleagues from The Institute of Archaeology, University College, London, who undertook a rescue dig on the site. This was to lead to further rescue digs, along the then proposed Rustington bypass.

These sites revealed previously unrecorded archaeological features, artefactual evidence from the Mesolithic, Bronze and Iron ages, and also from the Early Roman and later medieval periods. The finds included flint tools, implements, pots, cooking vessels, glass, coins and a copper alloy brooch. Post holes where their houses (some with chalk floors) had stood were also found. Most exciting were the traces of a Roman tidal mill and a causeway together with evidence of a fishery. Tree trunks that were dug up at the time were dated (by dendrochronology at The University of Sheffield) between 2835-2620 B.C.

Following the Roman withdrawal from these shores in A.D. 436, there came the Saxon invaders from Germany. They set up their settlements all along the coastal plains and river valleys. We have significant evidence of settlements established here in the village. It is possible that Rustington acquired its name about this time; it is certainly of Saxon origin. The Danes attempted frequent raids along this part of the coast. However the Saxon settlements here were hardly ever disturbed, and life stayed unchanged for centuries.

All was to change after the Norman Conquest in 1066. The village then became one of the estates given to Roger de Montgomerie by William the Conqueror. This brought the feudal system to Rustington, with a succession of Lords of the Manor.

Savaric Fitzcane was given the Manor by King Henry I in 1102. Savaric's grandson was confirmed in his tenure of the Manor by Richard I in 1190. Then in the 13th century there came the infamous de Bohuns, who were well known for abusing their rights, privileges and powers. After them the change of ownership becomes complicated, with descent through the female line. The Manor was divided into Rustington West Court and Rustington East Court.

Here is an extract from the archives of Althorp in Northamptonshire, later the home of Diana, Princess of Wales, appertaining to Rustington:

Deed No. 1470-2. Sale by way of mortgage by Sir John Dudley to Sir William Fitzwilliam, the kings cofferer, for £240, of half the Manor of Rustyngton. Date 6 Dec. 20 Hen. VIII (1528).

Some other well-known names associated with the lordship of the manors, were — Bramshott, Barford, Viscount de Lisle, Cooke, Bannister, Palmer, Sir Hugh Acland and the Dukes of Richmond and Norfolk. The last Lord of the Manor was William Kinleside Gratwick of Ham, Angmering — he died in 1862 and, with his death, the way of life in the village again changed.

19th- and 20th-Century Rustington

Rustington was always essentially a farming community, with several dairy farms and crop-producing farms. Midway through the 19th century, a combination of events changed the way of life of the folk of Rustington. The death of the last Lord of the Manor and the mechanisation of farming, which led to a loss of jobs for farm labourers, meant that new work had to be found.

At this time brickfields were being opened in Rustington, which required workers, and helped the employment situation. The first known brickfield was in 1867, east of Ash Lane, followed by several on both sides of Worthing Road. The last to open and,

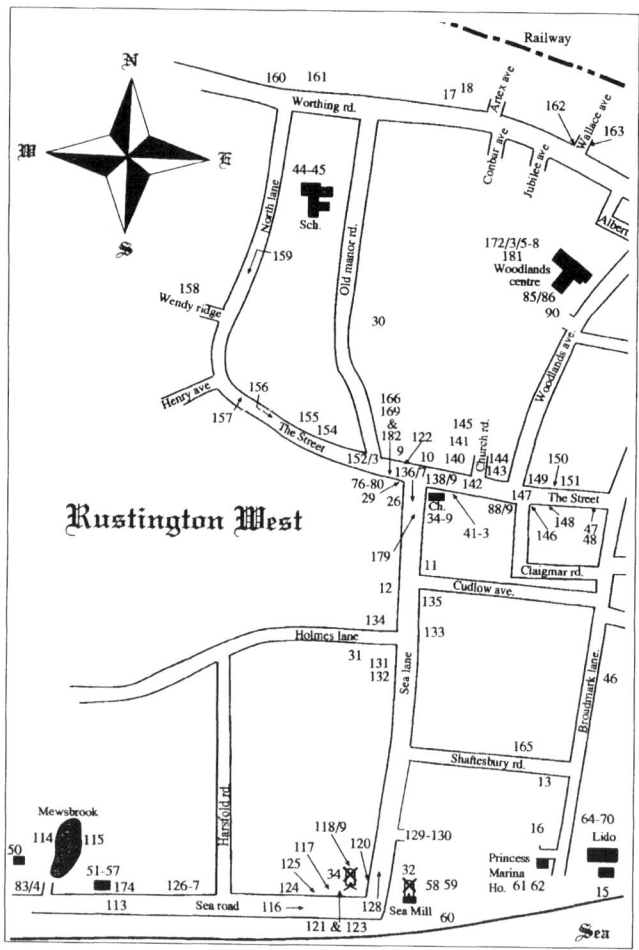

Figures on the maps correspond to illustrations throughout the book.

incidentally, the last to close, in 1948, was in North Lane. Mr. James Linfield of Littlehampton, one of the brickfield owners, had houses built for his workers in Worthing and Albert roads (c.1897-1907). The houses are still occupied.

The coming of the railway in 1846 was another factor in the change. This made the journey between London and the coast, much quicker and more convenient, so more people wanted to live here. The effect was that new houses had to be built, more bricks were needed, more labour required.

Rustington's first shop was opened by Mr. Simpson in 1846. He sold everything you could want, apart from drapery. The business was taken over by the Humphrey family. Mrs. Mary Ann Humphrey opened the first sub-post office in this shop in 1870, and in 1913 it became Rustington's first telephone call office. The shop stands in Sea Lane opposite the church, and the building is still there today.

Property developers also saw an opportunity in Rustington. Farm land was sold for building, and new roads and houses sprang up to cater for demand. Mr. Charles J. Drake built in Church Road and The Street, and Mr. Thomas Summers in Waverley, Glenville, Claigmar and Shaftesbury roads. They were among the first entrepreneurs to realise the potential of property.

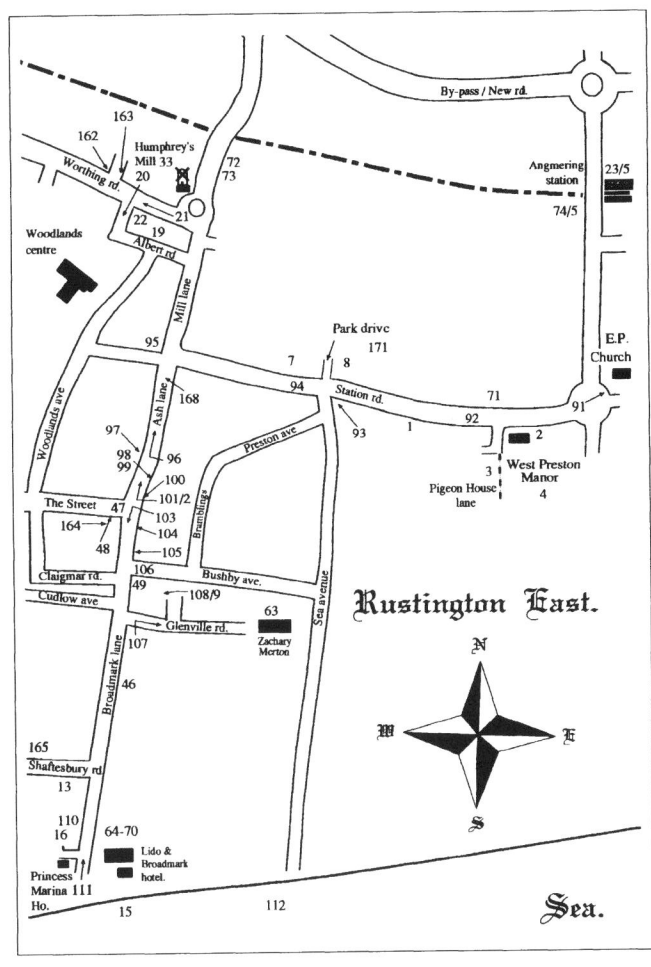

Mr. Summers was also responsible, during 1909, for building Broadway Mansions on the corner of The Street and Claigmar Road. These were the first purpose-built shops, over which nine apartments, on two storeys, were built. (These are now demolished and Sterling Parade is on the site.)

Some of the farmland was taken over by nurserymen. Over a dozen nurseries opened, producing glasshouse crops, which also eased the labour situation. All varieties of salad produce were grown; in particular, tomatoes and mushrooms, and exotic fruits and flowers.

Windmills

At one period Rustington had three working windmills. The earliest of them was situated to the north of the village, at the junction of Worthing Road, Mill Lane, and New Road. This mill, a post mill, had been known during its lifetime as Drewett's Mill, Humphrey's Mill and Bridge Mill, c.1615-1896.

A second mill, a turret post mill, stood at the south-east corner of Sea Lane (now Overstrand Estate). It was called Sea Mill, 1821-1913.

The third mill, which only stood for a short time (1848-57), was in the field on the west side of Sea Lane. This mill was an open trestle post mill, and was removed bodily to Fishbourne in October 1857.

Rustington Parish Church

It is possible that there was a church in Rustington before 1066. The very shape of the churchyard suggests that originally it was circular, typical of the Saxon period. The church would have been made of wattle and daub and thatched.

The first stone church would have been built sometime after 1066, under the jurisdiction of Earl Roger de Montgomerie. Earl Roger had a castle built for himself at nearby Arundel, when he became the first Earl of Arundel 1070-94. He imported the stone for his castle and churches from Caen in Normandy. Very little of this stone church now remains, having been altered and enlarged in the 12th and 13th centuries. The church, dedicated to St Peter and St Paul, is in a mixture of architectural styles, but is mostly Early English.

The tower dates from 1170 and is typical of its period. The date '1661', picked out in red brick near the top of the tower, indicates when the battlements were added.

The south arcade also dates from 1170 and is an excellent example of Transitional Norman architecture. The capitals on the pillars are very odd, and interesting.

The chancel is in the Early English style of about 1210. On the eastern face of the chancel arch are two shallow recesses that are worthy of note. There is a squint, which communicates with the Manorial/Lady Chapel. The chancel has an unusual, shuttered 'low-side' window. Apart from two circles of very old glass in a chancel window, all the stained glass is Victorian.

Two curious stone heads adorn the eastern arch into the Lady Chapel, from where you may also notice an opening near the chancel arch, with steps that once gave access to the rood loft.

The font is not the original one; this one dates from the 13th century. The font cover is Victorian and made of wood. Above hangs a gilded dove that is rather an unusual feature.

In 1992, the Lady Chapel floor was found to be suffering from wet rot and, while the floor was up for renovation, local archaeologists were invited to investigate. Six grave slabs were found, obviously not in their original resting places, and discovered beneath two of them was the original stone mensa [altar]. It had been smashed in half at the time of the Reformation, and the consecrational crosses, one at each corner, had been broken, though the central one was still clearly visible. The broken pieces were removed with difficulty, due to their weight and condition, and the altar top was then cleaned, measured, drawn and photographed. At a PCC meeting on 26 January 1993 it was resolved that the pieces of mensa/altar top should be placed under the new chapel floor, with an inspection cover over it. The historical connections with the Lady Chapel were thereby retained, and at the same time the stone was preserved.

The church has north and west porches of medieval origin and both have been skilfully restored.

More recently, during the 1939-45 war, the church was required to take part in the black-out. This was to stop light appearing outside, which might help enemy aircraft to navigate. Among the records of church expenditure for 1939-40 appears the following entry: 'To blacking out the church, and the necessary materials £2 5s. 1d. [225p]'

From the parish magazine during 1940, there was an important announcement to local blood donors:

> In the event of a serious local air-raid, all blood donors in class O are requested to watch the church tower for a red flag with a letter B. When this flag is raised, they shall report at Moot House, at ABC Corner, Rustington, at 10am the following morning without fail. Please note — the flag will be hoisted under police and military regulations.

Outside, on the north wall of the tower, is a single-handed clock dating from 1769. The clock was made in Marlborough, Wiltshire, and was used in Great Bedwyn church for about 100 years. In need of major repair, it was dismantled and removed, to be sold for what it could fetch — £2 0s. 0d. The purchaser was the Rev. E.J. Norris, vicar of a church in Reading, who happened to be a friend of one of the churchwardens of Rustington church. They needed a clock, so this ancient one was restored and fitted to the tower in 1905. The original circular iron face was removed and replaced by a square one, designed by Sir Ninian Comper. The present face is its fifth and is made of oak. The clock dial measures three feet in diameter. The solid brass hand is two feet long and weighs approximately 2lb. 6oz.

The picturesque lychgate was constructed from some old roof timbers, removed from the church at the time of its restoration in 1860. This replaced the five-bar farm gate which had stood there previously.

The church registers commenced in 1568. They show only too clearly when the Black Death swept through the village. The epidemic of 1597-99 caused 32 deaths to be recorded. In 1609, 21 villagers died, 15 of them within three months, while in 1670-71 the toll was 36 folk, as compared with an annual average death rate of four.

Rustington's Sunday School

In 1825, the Rev. J.C. Green started the first Sunday School in the village. It was held, not in the church as you would expect, but in the largest room at the *Lamb Inn*. The superintendent of the school was the pub landlord, Mr. Thomas Richardson. In 1844 the Sunday school was transferred to another unlikely home, the annexe of the village smithy, which stood on the corner of The Street and Broadmark Lane. The superintendent then was the village blacksmith, Mr. John Green. Here it remained until the Church School was built next to the church in 1859.

A Century for the National School

In 1859, the Rev. Henry J. Rush bought a piece of freehold land from the executors of the previous vicar, the Rev. J.C. Green, for £50. This land was situated between the old vicarage (now Abbots Lodge and Friars) and the churchyard. He employed a London architect, William Slater, to design a school and a school house and these plans are now deposited in the West Sussex Record Office at Chichester.

The Rev. Rush paid for the building himself, apart from a grant of £10 that he received from the Board of Education. When the building was completed on 5 June 1859, he conveyed, as a gift to the vicar, churchwardens and to the parish of Rustington, the school, the school house, and the land on which it stood.

Two date stones are set in the walls of the school house. One reads 'National School A.D. 1859', while the other reads 'E.M.R. A.D.1859'. These are the initials of the wife of the Rev. Rush, Elizabeth Martindale Rush, who died on 31 August 1859, aged 37.

The population in Rustington was about 345 at this time, and the school was built to accommodate 63 children. The average attendance was in fact 46 children, whose ages ranged from five to eleven years old.

By the turn of the century the population had almost doubled, so the school had to be enlarged. The cost of rebuilding had to be raised by the school itself. For several years they put on fund-raising concerts and plays, and the school building was enlarged in 1912, to accommodate 160 pupils.

During the six months of rebuilding, the children had their lessons at *The Lamb Inn* hall.

In 1939 a brand new school was built in North Lane. It included six classrooms, a hall, and cloakrooms to accommodate 240 pupils. When it opened in September 1939 there were 172 children on the roll.

This is not the end of the story of the old church school. It was called into service in 1949, when the North Lane School itself became overcrowded with 314 children on the roll. Two classrooms were brought back into use — a temporary measure that was to last for ten years!

Eventually new classrooms were built at North Lane in November 1960, and the classes at the old Church School finally ceased for ever. The original building is now The Rustington Church Hall.

Methodist Church Beginnings

On the death of the village blacksmith, his old 'smithy' at the corner of The Street and Broadmark Lane became empty and derelict for several years. A new blacksmith shop opened in Broadmark Lane, on the junction of what is now Bushby Avenue.

In 1875 a small group of Methodists began to worship together in a small cottage (now demolished) called Hedgerville in Broadmark Lane. This was the home of Charles and Louisa Hedger and William and Elizabeth Gates. Within two years this small group had raised sufficient money to buy the 'old smithy'.

Snewin's, builders from Littlehampton, converted the smithy into a chapel. The annexe, which at one time had housed the parish church Sunday School, became a Sunday School for the Methodists. Snewin's made five memorial stones, as well as 'dressing up the chapel on Easter Monday 1878, for a tea party, on the opening of the chapel'.

The membership of the Primitive Methodist Chapel grew quickly from the days of the early pioneers and a new church building became a necessity. The chapel was also a traffic hazard, as it stood well out into a busy main road.

The Summers family donated land in Claigmar Road to the Methodists. A building permit was granted, and the new Methodist church was then built. On 29 May 1952, the congregation held a brief farewell service in the old Primitive Chapel. They then walked the few hundred yards to the new church for a service of thanksgiving, which was conducted by the Rev. Dr. W.E. Sangster.

A small part of the old chapel was preserved, however, when one of the original five memorial stones, dated 1878, that had been laid by a Mrs. Mason, was set into the present building.

Distinctive Properties Past and Present

Mewsbrook House was built in 1870 by Robert Bushby of Littlehampton for Mrs. Louis Barnes. It was a large castellated building, with extensive grounds, and stood just west of the Mewsbrook swamp on Sea Road, at this period within the boundary of Rustington. The Barnes family occasionally hosted parties in their house and grounds for inmates of the East Preston Union Workhouse, also known as North View and locally as 'The Spike'.

Mrs. Bland purchased Mewsbrook House in 1923-4, and had the building extended in the same eccentric style. She then opened it as a modern hotel, calling it the *Rustington Towers Hotel*. Unfortunately, most of the hotel was destroyed by fire in 1935. There were plans to rebuild it, but they had to be shelved, as findings from test bores taken on the site showed running blue river mud at a depth of 30 feet. The idea of rebuilding was abandoned and the small section of the old hotel that had escaped the fire was demolished. Part of the overgrown garden can still be seen behind the pumping station, including a giant mulberry tree.

In 1894, a large area of land along the Sea Road, west of the Mewsbrooks, was bought by Sir Henry Harben of Warnham. He employed the architect Frederick Wheeler in 1897 to design a convalescent home. It was to have its own concert hall, electricity supply, steam laundry, bacterial drainage treatment system, home farm, and a lodge on a 17½-acre site. So Sir Henry Harben, who was Master of The Worshipful Company of Carpenters, was the founder of one of the most complete convalescent homes of its kind. It is the largest building in the district and, from all points of view, one of the finest. After the outbreak of the Second World War, the home was closed. It was suggested that it should be used as a military hospital, but this was considered inadvisable, owing to the possible danger of the district being in the direct line of an invasion. It re-opened as a convalescent home during the summer of 1948, and has recently celebrated its centenary.

Further eastwards along the sea front, where the Overstrand Estate now stands, was the Millfield Convalescent Home. The five-and-a-half-acre site was bought by the Metropolitan Asylums Board in 1903. Four large buildings were opened as a seaside home for children on 6 April 1904. Later it was taken over by the London County Council, when it became a convalescent home for children suffering from tuberculosis. Dr. Last of Littlehampton was the appointed doctor at the home, which he visited daily. He also played the part of Father Christmas annually for the children. The home was closed and requisitioned by the military at the beginning of the Second World

War. It was left in a derelict state and was not to be used again. In 1958 it was demolished.

However, its final moment of glory was when it was used as one of the timing points in attempts on the world air-speed records. The first, on 7 September 1946 by Group Captain E.M. Donaldson, flying a Gloster Meteor IV, achieved a speed of 615.78 mph, breaking the previous record that had stood at 606.38 mph. The second occasion was on 7 September 1953, when Squadron Leader Neville Duke, OBE, DSO, DFC with two bars and AFC, broke the record again, in a Hawker Hunter mkIII at an average speed of just over 727 mph.

In 1996, to celebrate these two achievements and 50 years to the day after the first record, Rustington Parish Council arranged a suitable ceremony. The special guest, Squadron Leader Neville Duke, unveiled the commemorative plaque, and an invited audience and a large crowd gathered on the sea shore to watch the unveiling. This was followed by a flying display by Capt. S. Hodgkins in a Gloster Meteor and Capt. Brian Henwood in a Hawker Hunter, planes similar to those which broke the records over the original course.

A little further eastwards from this point towards Broadmark Lane is Princess Marina House, earlier known as the Newton Driver Services Club. This was opened in April 1947 by H.R.H. The Duke of Edinburgh, when many Rustington folk turned out to welcome him to the village. The club was founded by Mrs. Newton Driver, O.B.E., in memory of her husband, for the use of officers of the Royal Navy, the Army and the Royal Air Force. The name was changed to Princess Marina House when the Princess visited the club in 1962. It became a home for ex-RAF personnel in 1969, when the complex was taken over by the RAF Benevolent Fund.

Many people born in the years between 1946-79, whose parents lived between Bognor Regis and Worthing, may be surprised to learn from birth certificates, that they were born in Rustington. This is because The Zachary Merton Maternity Hospital in Rustington covered this catchment area.

The name Zachary Merton is that of a generous philanthropist. He left a large sum of money, on the death of his wife, to be used for the founding of convalescent homes, and Rustington was the site of one of these homes. The architects were Messrs. Stanley Hall, Easton and Robertson of London, and it was built, at a cost of £32,896 by Messrs. Chapman, Lowry and Puttick of Haslemere, as a convalescent home for mothers, babies and their toddlers, and was opened on 28 April 1937.

Later, it became a maternity hospital and held an enviable reputation for over 30 years. Eventually it was scaled down and finally closed as a maternity unit in June 1979. The building re-opened in November of that same year as a community hospital.

During 1936, 'The Lido', a first-class holiday complex, was established in the village. It possessed a ballroom, lecture/conference hall, floodlit swimming pool, children's pool, outdoor roller skating rink, bowling greens, and tennis courts, to name a few of the amenities. This was all set in 40 acres of ground, with flower gardens and coloured fountains. *The Lido*, however, did not hold a licence to sell alcoholic drinks, which was catered for at the adjacent *Broadmark Hotel*, built for the owner Mr. Sydney Jones at the same time.

During the 1939-45 War, like all other large properties in Rustington, The Lido and the *Broadmark Hotel* were requisitioned by the military. On the run-up to D-Day on 6 June 1944, thousands of Americans troops arrived in this country to take part in this momentous operation. Mr. Rockall, the local troop billeting officer, was asked to prepare the whole complex to house the first troops to arrive. While the American troops were stationed there, in 1943 they gave a large Christmas party for the children of servicemen in the village.

After the war, in 1947 The Lido was sold to the Workers Travel Association (W.T.A.). Ten years later it was renamed Mallon Dene, after Sir J. J. Mallon, head of the W.T.A. The holiday complex was eventually demolished in 1968, and the site is now occupied by the Mallon Dene Estate. The *Broadmark Hotel* continued in use until 1984, when that also was demolished, and the 'Broadmark Beach' flats now occupy this site.

Lying almost opposite the old Pigeon House Lane, that is, next to West Preston Manor, there once stood a fine old flint building called Walnut Tree Cottage. Documents appertaining to it, dating from 1615, revealed that in the early 18th century it was an inn, known by its sign as the *New Inn*. (The sign in those days was a brush or branch of a tree, tied on a pole above the inn door, an elementary form of today's inn signs.) This was probably the first ale house in Rustington. It was reputedly the meeting place of the Rustington band of smugglers known as 'The Ragman Totts':

> A few days since, Messrs. Heaseman and Roberts, revenue officers at Rustington, seized from the Ragman Totts company of smugglers, 49 casks of cognac, brandy and geneva, and lodged the same in the Arundel Custom House. 5 Nov. 1787.

After the *New Inn* ceased trading in 1829 it was sold, and became a family home once again, named Walnut Tree Cottage. Finally West Sussex County Council bought it in 1949 for £1,050. Being in a bad state of repair by then, it was demolished soon after for road improvements.

Rustington now has three public houses, namely the *Windmill Inn*, the *Fletcher Arms* and the *Lamb Inn*. The *Windmill Inn* to the north east of the village derives its name from the mill that stood opposite it. The licence was transferred from the *New Inn* in Station Road when it closed in 1829. A new *Windmill Inn* was purpose-built in 1909, replacing the original *Windmill Inn*. The old inn was converted into two cottages, known as Windmill Cottages 1 and 2 and the new inn stands just south of the old inn. The walls of its old bowling alley can still be seen in the garden of the cottages.

The *Fletcher Arms*, standing near Angmering Station, was converted from a house called Munmere Cottage, where J. Warr(en) a fly proprietor lived and at one time had his livery stables. In 1933 the cottage was extended and converted into a public house by Messrs. Henty and Constable. It was named *The Fletcher Arms* after Sir Henry Aubrey Fletcher of Ham Manor. The inn licence was not new but was transferred from the *Red Lion Inn* at Angmering village. Mr. and Mrs. M.H. Thomas opened the premises for business in February 1934, and the pub remained in the hands of the Thomas family for 44 years.

The *Lamb Inn*, standing opposite the parish church, could be a contender for the first pub in the village. It is not clear from existing records whether it was opened in 1779 or 1809, but we think 1809 is more likely, when James Richardson the owner took out an extra mortgage of £400. He was also a cordwainer, combining the two trades to make ends meet. Documents of 1779 refer to a cellar in the building, so perhaps the inn was already in existence then. Would an old cottage *c.*1660 have had a cellar? This inn was also used as the local early type of bank, a venue for land and property auctions, and the home of the Sunday School.

The old *Lamb Inn* was a long, low single-storey building, which was demolished and replaced by a new purpose-built inn during 1902. This had a large adjoining hall, which was used for various functions, including smoking concerts, wedding receptions, The Ancient Order of Foresters' meetings, school classes and occasionally as a mortuary. Later it was used for billiards and snooker, and it had three full-size tables. The hall was pulled down in 1959 for road widening, which incidentally never materialised. The *Lamb Inn* has undergone many modernisations since then.

*   *   *

It comes as a surprise to many people to learn that there was an air station in Rustington during the First World War; it was, in fact, an American aerodrome. Building only began in 1917, one year before the end of the war, so it never had time to become fully operational. However, aircraft used it for flying in spares and equipment. Over 40 per cent of the projects were complete by early 1918. It was to have been the base for American personnel to train on the Handley Page 0/400, a night bomber with a 100ft. wing span, before leaving for active service in France. The grass runway ran from north to south, so that aircraft could take off towards the sea. The main entrance to the airfield was from Station Road, now the entrance to Sea Avenue (Sea Estate). The airfield had its own railway siding, a branch line off the main south-coast railway that ran between Brighton and Portsmouth. The line served the mess and barracks as well as the airfield and crossed Station Road near Sea Avenue.

Only two airfield buildings remain in situ: 'Fairholme', a bungalow converted from the guard house, at the entrance to Sea Avenue; and 'Nortons'/'Galleons', a bungalow from a converted salvage shed, in Preston Avenue. The arrival of so many American and Canadian troops to work on the aerodrome must have had a considerable impact on the quiet, sleepy village life in Rustington.

Apart from the war years, building development within the parish has never ceased, and the population has grown to over 12,500 from 616 in 1901.

Rustington is still primarily a residential area, favoured by young and old alike. It retains its old-world cottages, to which have been added bungalows, modern blocks of flats, as well as a superb shopping centre. Despite extensive development, it still has its former charm and jealously guards its special village identity.

m
if

sh

3 *(left)* Mr. Thomas Bushby watches while his men are sheep shearing in one of his barns on the manor.

4 *(below left)* The Shepherd, together with a flock of his sheep, on West Preston Manor Farm.

5 *(below)* Mr. Richard Henson poses by his steam plough tackle, while his sons Noah and James carry on work with the other farm labourers.

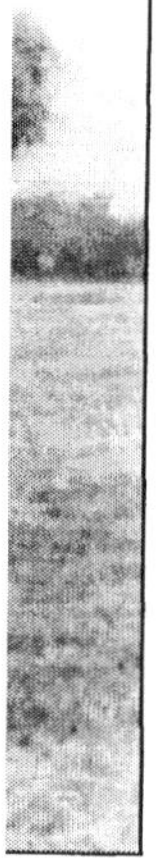

of the
— i.e.

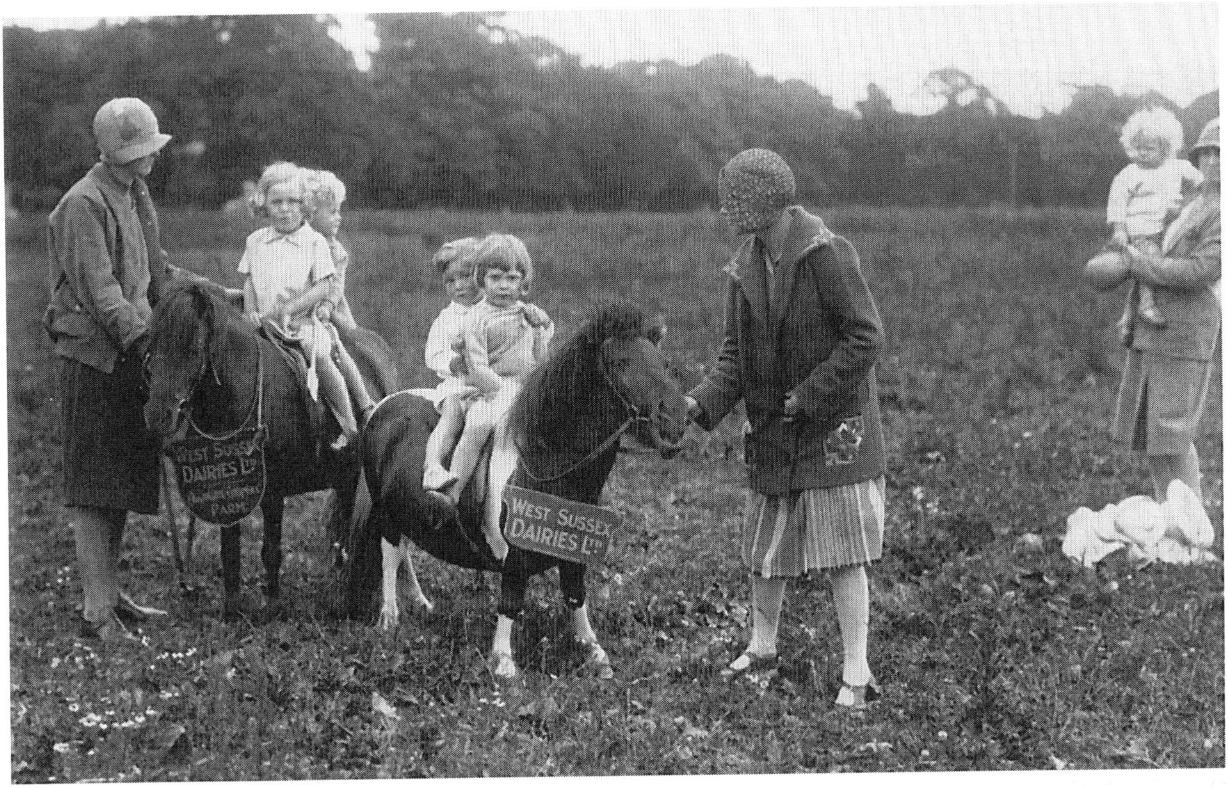
WEST SUSSEX
DAIRIES Ltd
FARM
WEST SUSSEX
DAIRIES Ltd

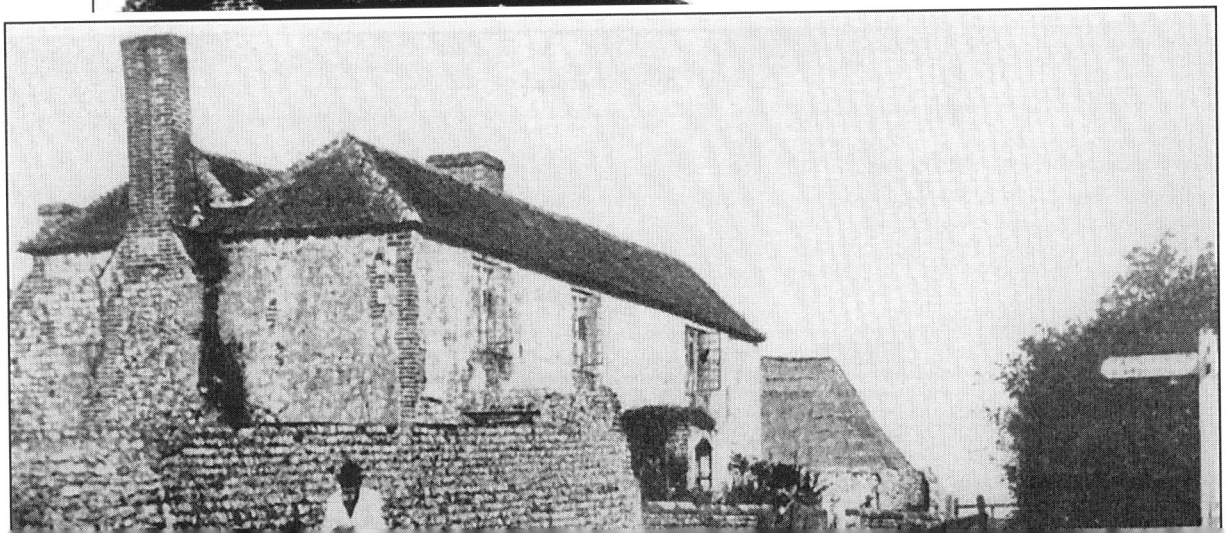

10 *(left)* Quaker Smith's Farm, *c.*1890. All that now remains of this farm is the cottage on the left known as Church Farm Cottage (rear view). The farmyard has been used as a builder's yard for many years, both by C.J. Drake and Hall & Co. A small parade of shops occupies the site of the old barns.

11 *(below left)* Cudlow Farm. This 1899 picture shows Dorothy Cobden carrying her younger brother, Richard, standing in the doorway of their father's farmhouse. Her father was cousin of Richard Cobden, of Corn Law fame. They took over the farm from the Newman family in 1862. The house and barn are still in existence, although Cudlow Avenue was cut through the farmyard in 1930.

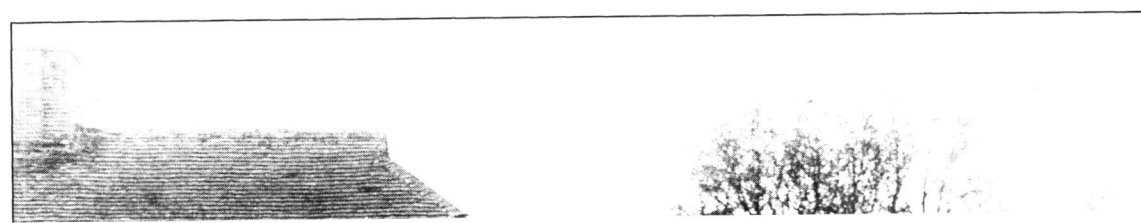

12 *(below)* Hobbs Farm, *c.*1900. The entrance gates to the farm are on the left of this picture. The house dates from 1690. Roger and Elizabeth Barwick had it built to replace an existing house. Elizabeth Barwick inherited the land and property from her father John Upperton. The farm takes its name from the Hobbs family who were the owners in the 18th century. Cudlow Farm and barns can be seen on the right.

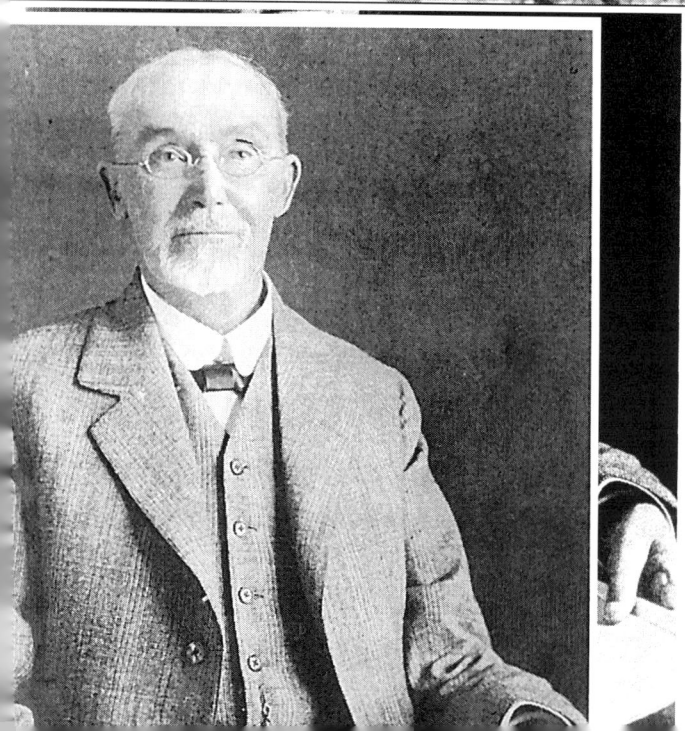

ower',
the
mers'

14 Mr. Thomas Summers (1851-1933), property developer and land-owner, lived at Normanhurst, Broadmark Lane (house now demolished). He built the Glenville, Waverley, and Claigmar Road houses and also Shaftesbury House. He built the Broadway

m
t

u

ctoria
Mrs.
. The

cte

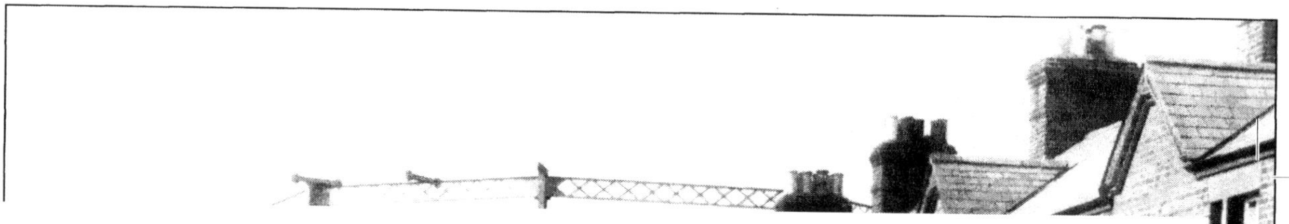

gone.

e also

23 *(left)* London, Brighton & South Coast Railway. The attractive waiting room and signal box on the down line at Angmering Station, *c*.1908.

24 *(below left)* Angmering Station *c*.1912 shows six of the regular staff. (From left to right) Ted Leggat, clerk / porter, George Leggat, clerk / porter, Bill Thorpe, signalman, Fred Lucas, porter, Billy Moon, porter, Horace Hayward, Station Master.

25 *(below)* The Hoover Express pulling away from Angmering Station. A convention had been held at The Lido Rustington, 1938. (Courtesy of Middleton Press.)

. He
from

27 The postmen: (from left to right) Bill Edmunds, Mr. Corney, Jack Greysmark and Jack MacDonald, *c.*1905. The mail was sorted and then delivered from Angmering Station, which had its own postmark.

dening

30 Dingley Nursery, Christmas Day 1951. Jack Kessler, owner, is seen watering some of the plants at his nursery in Old Manor Road. Very few nursery pictures now exist.

31 Smuggler's Nursery, Holmes Lane, drawn by Charles Hunnibal, Mrs. Ma___ brother, showing some of the layout of the r___ Mr. Manning was the owner from Novemb___ to its closure in 1964. Chanctonbury and Cove Road now run through the site.

SMUGGLER'

for—

FRUIT

FLOWERS

VEGETABLES

—

FLORAL
WORK

—

Phone:
RUSTINGTON
696

RUSTINGTON · SUSSEX

ght of
r. The

ted by
built
indmill

Inn at this time. The existing *Windmill Inn* was built in 1909. The miller's house was demolished *c*.1960; the adjoining 'new' miller's cottage is still there but much rebuilt. The windmill itself was taken down in 1896.

do
sh
't'

ar
d,
ne
ng
th
er
m
re
ve

35 *(left)* Rustington parish church in 1854. This picture was taken by Dr. Diamond before the church restoration took place. Here we see the old five-barred gate that served as the entrance to the churchyard. The lych-gate that stands here today was erected in 1860, using old roof timbers from the church.

36 *(below left)* Church interior in 1854, looking east, showing the old box pews and the east windows when they still contained clear glass. This picture was taken by Dr. Diamond.

37 *(below)* Church interior, *c.*1905, showing oil lamp lighting, new pews and stained glass. The chancel arch with embellishment, carried out under the direction of Mr. N.J. Comper, depicts the Ten Commandments. (*Parish Magazine*, May 1941.)

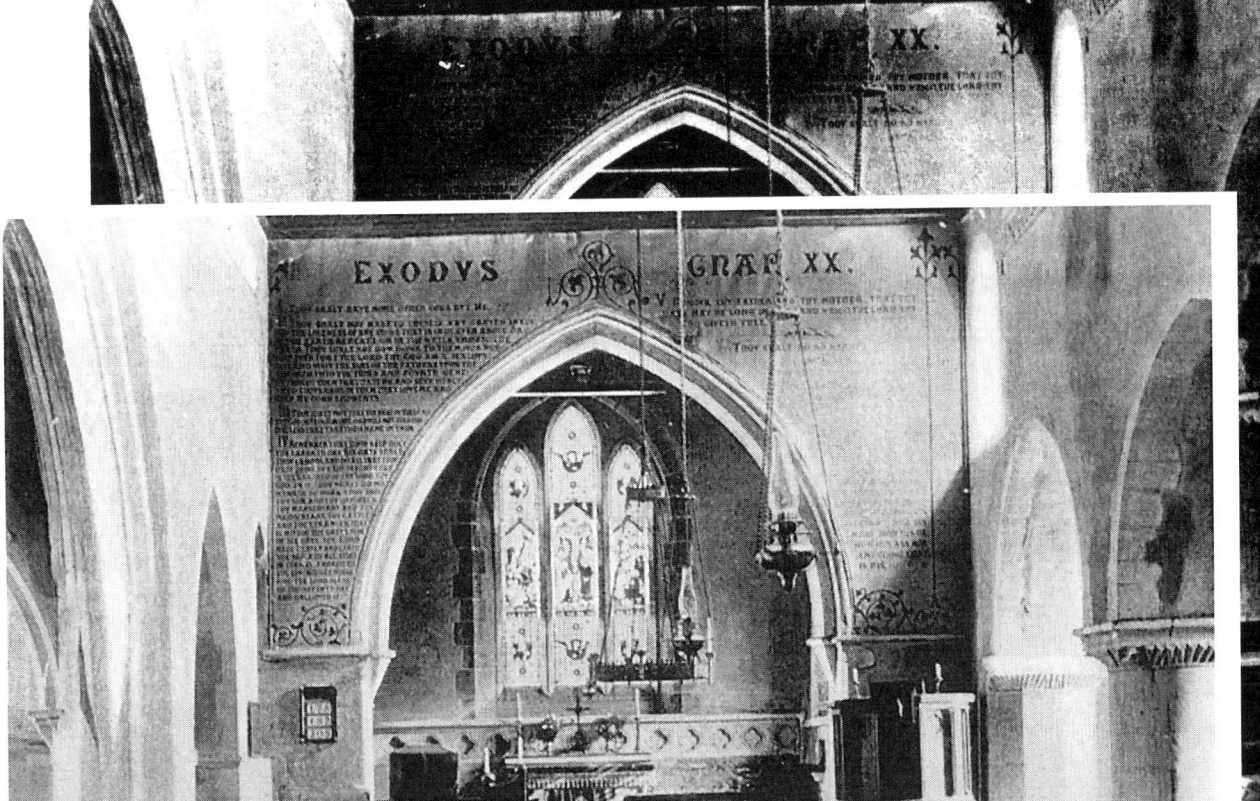

essary

39 Rustington Parish Church, c.1890. Children gather for some occasion outside the west gate. The ancient elm tree (left) stood by a stile, where a footpath led to Worthing Road and Bridge Mill. Church Road was built here in 1897.

wh
vica

school
picture.

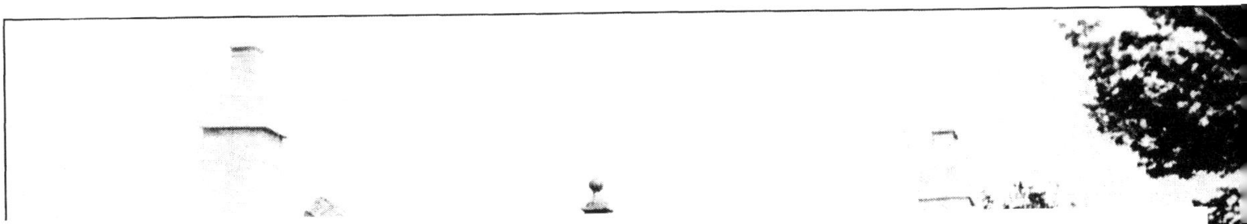

Field. Local garden and church fêtes were held here. Today it is the site of Sterling Parade.

olven,
Nellie
Alfred

over
. Mr.

·Rustington·Convalescent·Home·
·Littlehampton· ·for·Working·Men·

·Rustington·Convalescent·Home·
·Littlehampton· ·for·Working·Men·

March 20ᵗʰ 1897.

·Programme·
·of·the·
·Opening·Ceremony·

52 Opening ceremony programme, when the Right Rev. The Lord Bishop of Chichester opened the Rustington Convalescent Home on 20 March 1897.

53 Rustington Convalescent Home, *c.*1905. Note the pony and trap transport.

in

e th

and
urch
the

58 *(top right)* Millfield Convalescent Home, 1903. Men at work, building the home. Note the large work force, and the wooden scaffolding, which was roped together. It opened as a sunshine home for children.

59 *(right)* Millfield Convalescent Home, 1903-58. It occupied 5½ acres of land north of the old Sea Mill. It could accommodate 100 patients in its four large wings. It was requisitioned during 1939/45 war by the military, and was left derelict and demolished in 1958.

RUSTINGTON
PARISH
COUNCIL
IN COMMEMORATION OF
WORLD AIR SPEED RECORDS
SET UP OFF-SHORE
OPPOSITE THIS POINT ON
7 SEPTEMBER 1946
AND
7 SEPTEMBER 1953
7 SEPTEMBER 1996

...laque
...or in
...iming
...gston.

...emony
...1 1949.

62 HRH Prince Philip talks to the officer in charge of the local Sea Cadets, during their inspection, at the opening ceremony of the Newton Driver Services Club.

osp

ke

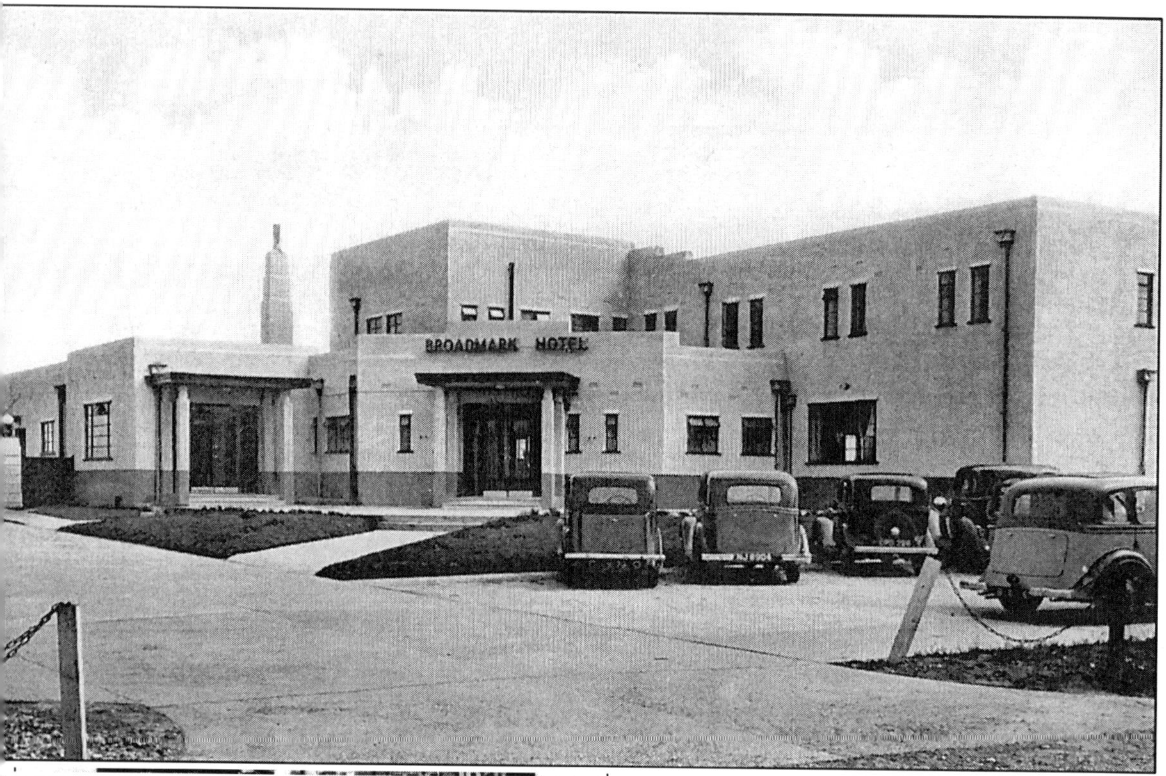
BROADMARK HOTEL

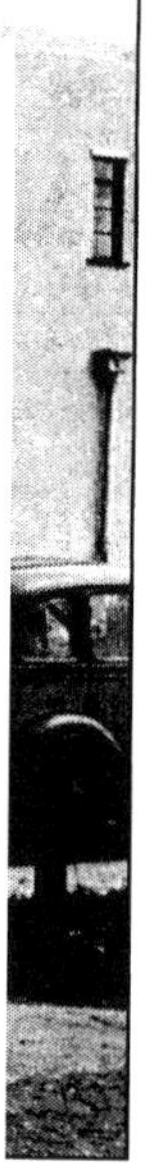

front

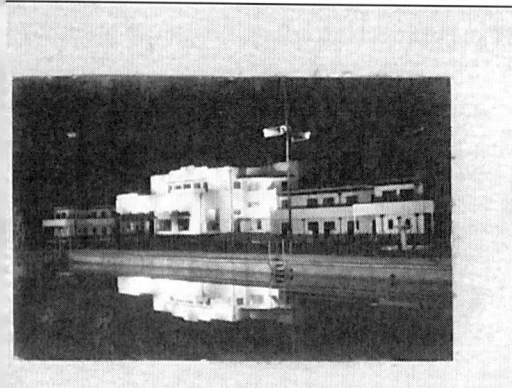

DINNER DANCE
AND
CABARET
ON THE OCCASION
OF THE OPENING
OF THE
RUSTINGTON LIDO

66 Programme and menu for the opening dinner dance and cabaret, 22 May 1936. It contains the signatures of

67 The Lido holiday camp opened in 1936 with a dinner dance. This photo shows the dining room before the first guests arrived and the waitresses are standing by. The Lido could accommodate 450 guests and 50 staff and had 236 bedrooms.

71 *The New Inn*, possibly Rustington's first beer house, 1778-1829, owned by James Burfield. It was sited opposite West Preston Manor. The original cottage was let in 1615 to John Hebenden, a blacksmith, at a rent of one peppercorn for a term of 10,000 years. Bought by Margaret Bushby in 1829, it reverted to a cottage (Walnut Tree). Eventually in 1949 it was bought for £1,050 by West Sussex County Council and it was then demolished for road widening.

owner.

73 The 'new' *Windmill Inn* was built in 1909 in Mil where mine host was Herbert Ralph Rooker

uilding

TELEPHONE 27 RUSTINGTON
DISTANCE

CARS HIRE
TELEPHONE 27 RUSTINGTON
DISTANCE

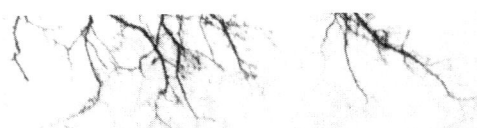

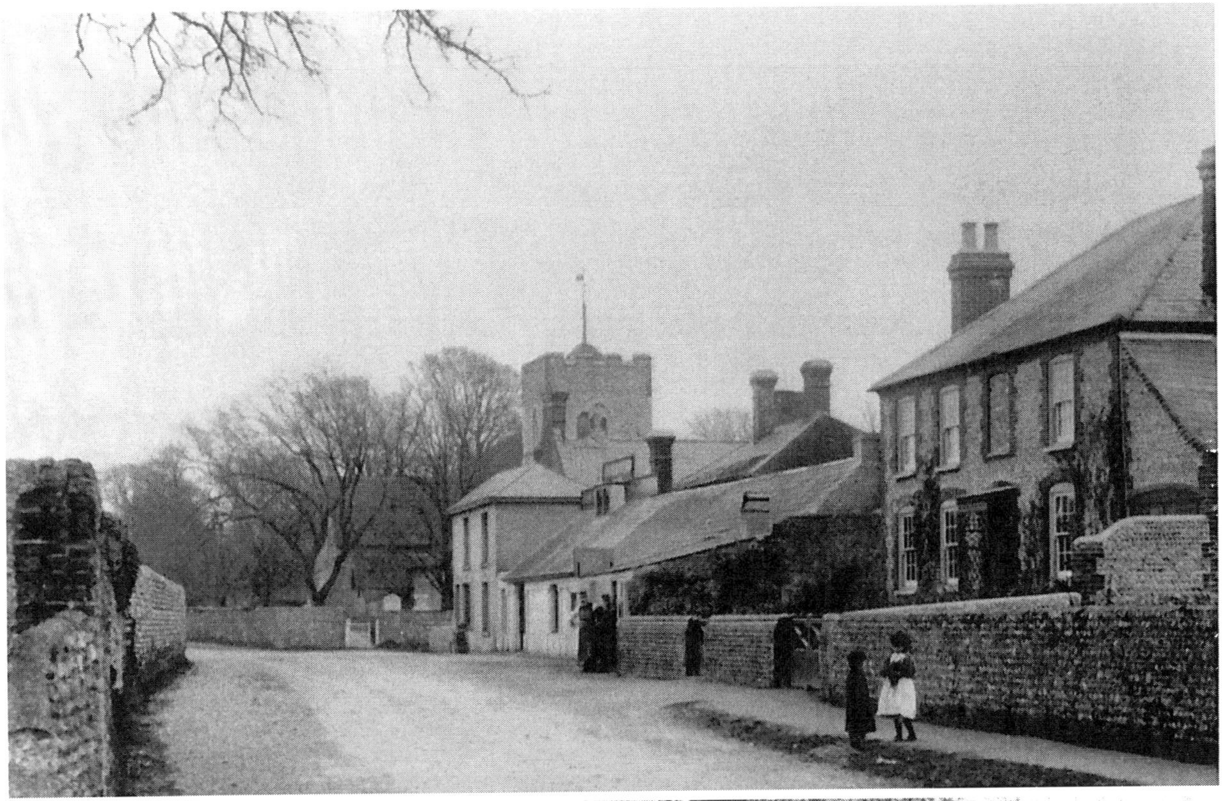

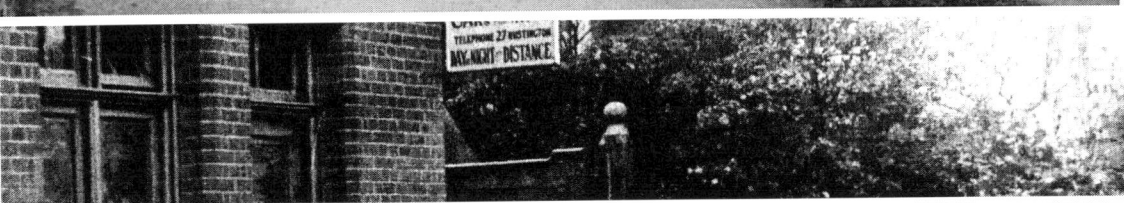

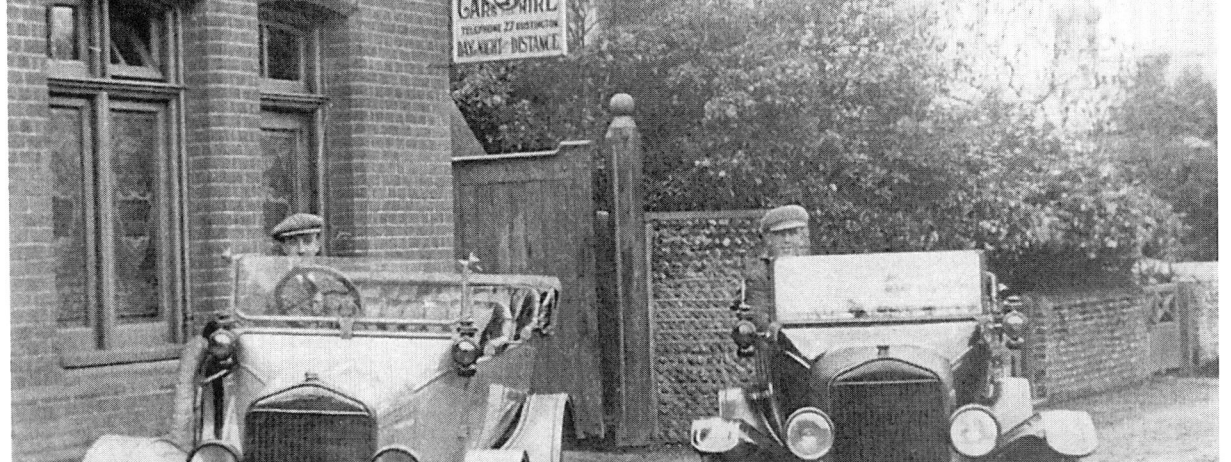

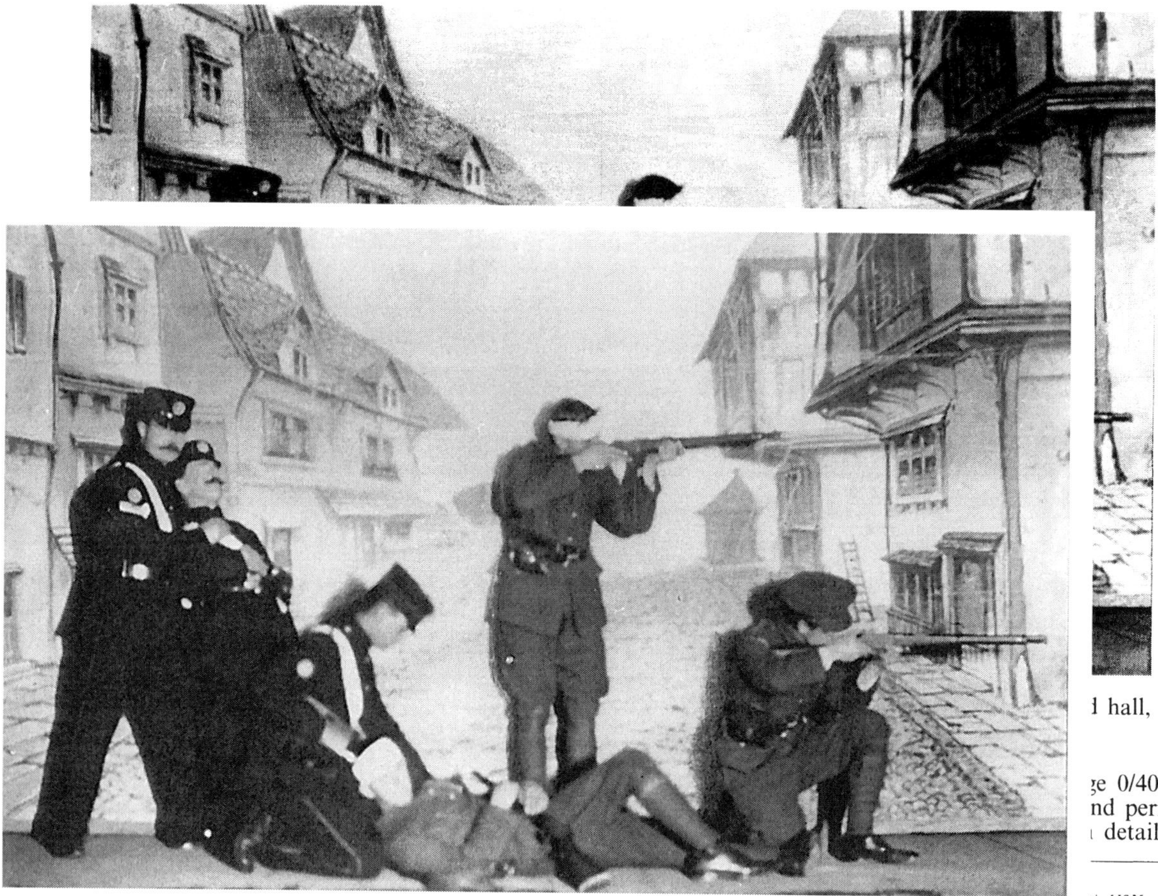

…d hall,

…ge 0/400 night
…nd permission
… detail.

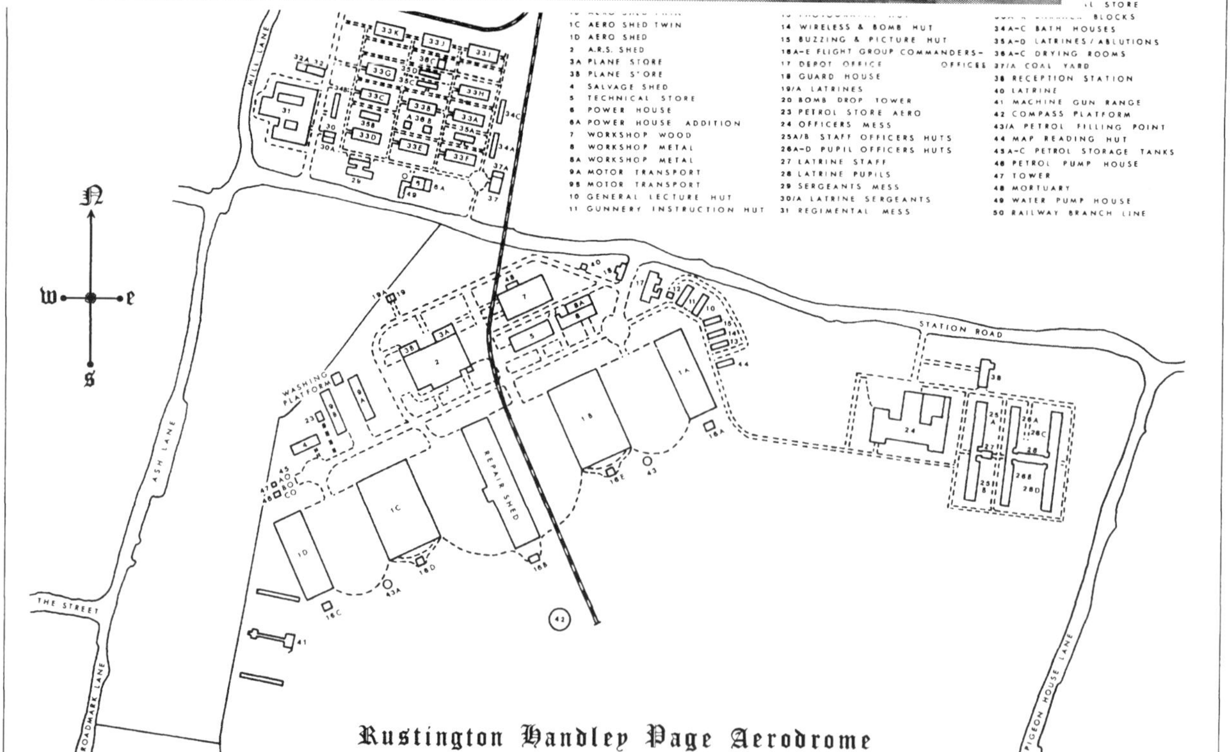

1C AERO SHED TWIN
1D AERO SHED
2 A.R.S. SHED
3A PLANE STORE
3B PLANE S'ORE
4 SALVAGE SHED
5 TECHNICAL STORE
6 POWER HOUSE
6A POWER HOUSE ADDITION
7 WORKSHOP WOOD
8 WORKSHOP METAL
8A WORKSHOP METAL
9A MOTOR TRANSPORT
9B MOTOR TRANSPORT
10 GENERAL LECTURE HUT
11 GUNNERY INSTRUCTION HUT
14 WIRELESS & BOMB HUT
15 BUZZING & PICTURE HUT
16A–E FLIGHT GROUP COMMANDERS–OFFICES
17 DEPOT OFFICE
18 GUARD HOUSE
19/A LATRINES
20 BOMB DROP TOWER
23 PETROL STORE AERO
24 OFFICERS MESS
25A/B STAFF OFFICERS HUTS
26A–D PUPIL OFFICERS HUTS
27 LATRINE STAFF
28 LATRINE PUPILS
29 SERGEANTS MESS
30/A LATRINE SERGEANTS
31 REGIMENTAL MESS
…L STORE
… BLOCKS
34A–C BATH HOUSES
35A–D LATRINES / ABLUTIONS
36A–C DRYING ROOMS
37/A COAL YARD
38 RECEPTION STATION
40 LATRINE
41 MACHINE GUN RANGE
42 COMPASS PLATFORM
43/A PETROL FILLING POINT
44 MAP READING HUT
45A–C PETROL STORAGE TANKS
46 PETROL PUMP HOUSE
47 TOWER
48 MORTUARY
49 WATER PUMP HOUSE
50 RAILWAY BRANCH LINE
MILL LANE
STATION ROAD
WASHING PLATFORM
REPAIR SHED
ASH LANE
THE STREET
BROADMARK LANE
PIGEON HOUSE LANE

Rustington Handley Page Aerodrome

AMERICAN AIRFORCE TRAINING DEPOT 1918

SITE PLAN

82 The Handley Page 0/400 night bomber had a 100ft wingspan. This photo was taken from the microfilm.

83 Sea View Café, at the corner of Hendon and Sea Road, was used as a canteen for troop the Second World War.

CANTEEN
FOR THE SERVICES

HOT LUNCH

llfield

s was

ar

LIMIT OF
OPEN BEACH
DANGER FROM MINES

who

𝔙illage 𝔚ar 𝔐emorial

✤

This Memorial, which bears the names of those people of Rustington who gave their lives in the two Wars 1914-1918 and 1939-1945, is now to be unveiled in the presence of representatives of all sections of the Village community this sixth day of July, 1952.

**LIVE THOU FOR ENGLAND
WE FOR ENGLAND DIED**

HYMN (A.M. No. 165): Oh, God, our Help in ages past. (Led by Choir)

PRAYER

BIBLE READING: Wisdom of Solomon, Chap. 3, verses 1-9

SPEECH OF INTRODUCTION BY CHAIRMAN

SPEECH AND UNVEILING BY ADMIRAL C. CASLON, C.B., C.B.E., R.N.

LAYING OF WREATH BY REPRESENTATIVE BODIES

LAST POST (Standards " DIP ")

SHORT SILENCE

REVEILLE (Standards " CARRY ")

NATIONAL ANTHEM. (Led by Choir)

bas
ow

vil

laque
time

verge,
impse

the parish council considered buying
Whitecroft for a village centre, but t
was rejected. Church Farm Estate is
this site.

98 The village 'bobby' in 1908. The
council thought it expedient to have
constable stationed in the village. F
see him outside Mrs. Upfield's groce

t is
run
and

100 Westminster Bank was the first bank to open for business in Rustington, in 1935. It was alongside Welling's the estate agent, in a room of the old house called The Matthew's and it stood opposite the junction of The Street and Ash Lane, now part of Broadmark Parade. The Bank

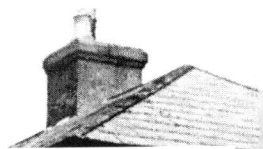

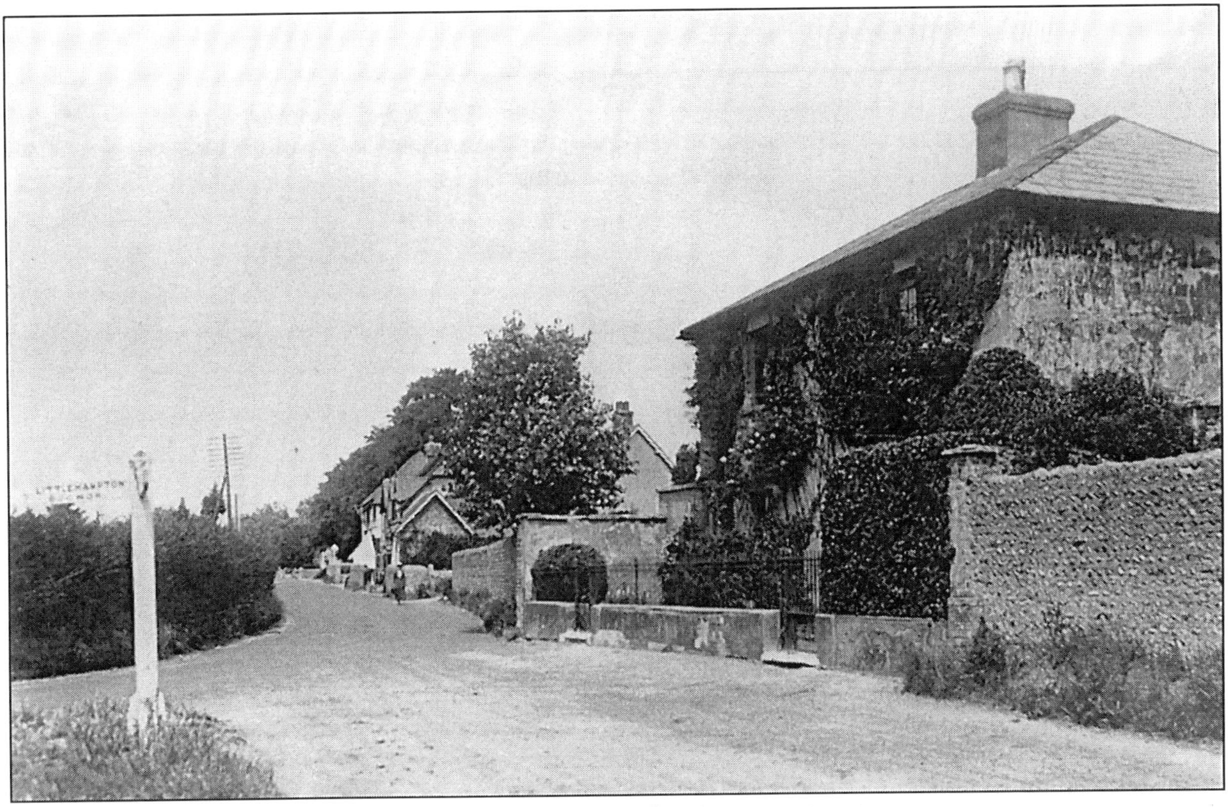

LITTLEHAMPTON
BOGNOR

ESTATE
AGENTS

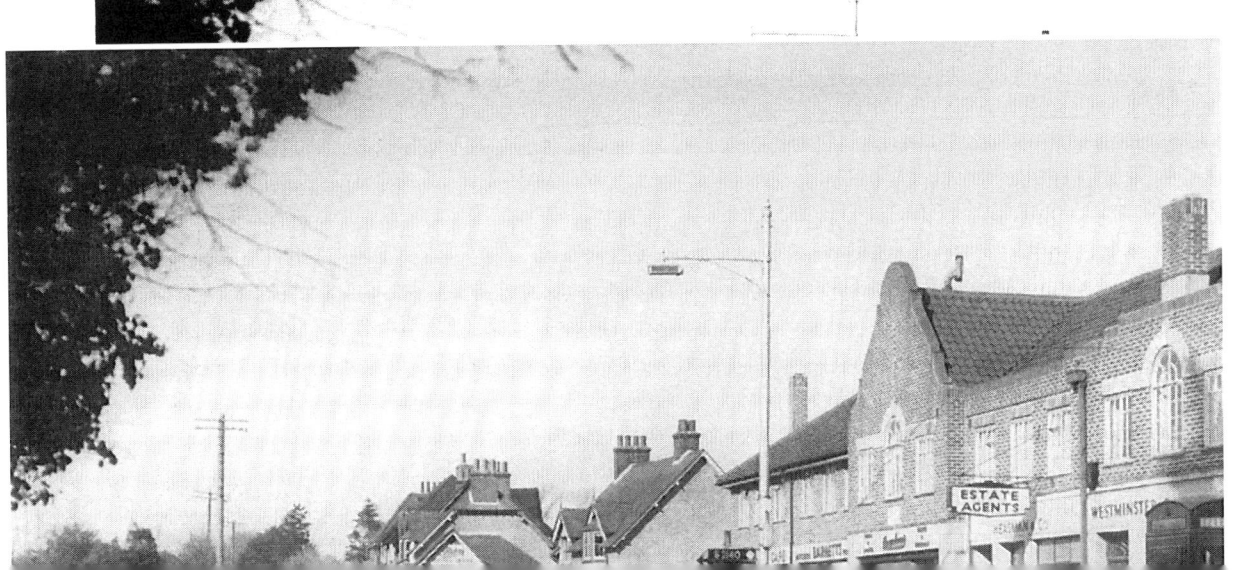

roof
shop,

time.
, was

106 Bushby Avenue as it looked in the 1920s. It derived its name from the land-owner, Thomas Bushby of W Preston manor.

village

ed the

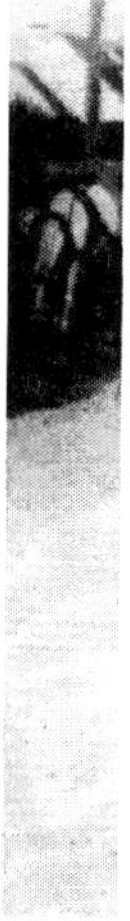

s lane
ay at

right
is Normanhurst, home of Thomas Summers, the builder and developer. It is said that Mrs. Summers named the roads and houses from books she had read. The origin of 'Claigmar' Road is unknown, but it is understood to be the only one in England.

114 *(left)* The Mewsbrook swamp in 1935. This was the delta of the river Arun centuries ago. This part of Rustington was taken over by Littlehampton in 1933 and was turned into a boating lake and pleasure garden.

115 *(below left)* The creation of the Mewsbrook boating lake. During drainage work a 'dug-out' boat was uncovered, and also possible signs of a Roman harbour.

116 *(below)* Sea Road in the 1920s. The high wall on the left was in front of Seafield Court which stood close the junction of Sea Lane.

19th
time

here
s on

122 *(above right)* South Acton scouts with their hand cart outside Morrallee's newspaper shop, next to Rustington Manor House. The billboard advertises 'Law of the Lawless' at the Electric Palace Cinema, Terminus Road, Littlehampton.

123 *(right)* On fatigues at the cook house, the cook was

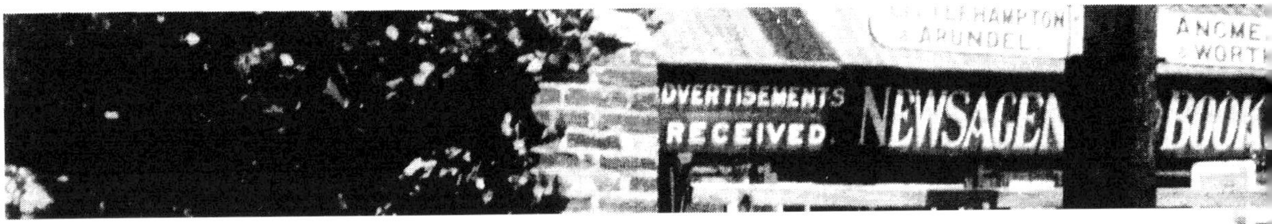
ARUNDEL
DVERTISEMENTS
RECEIVED
NEWSAGEN

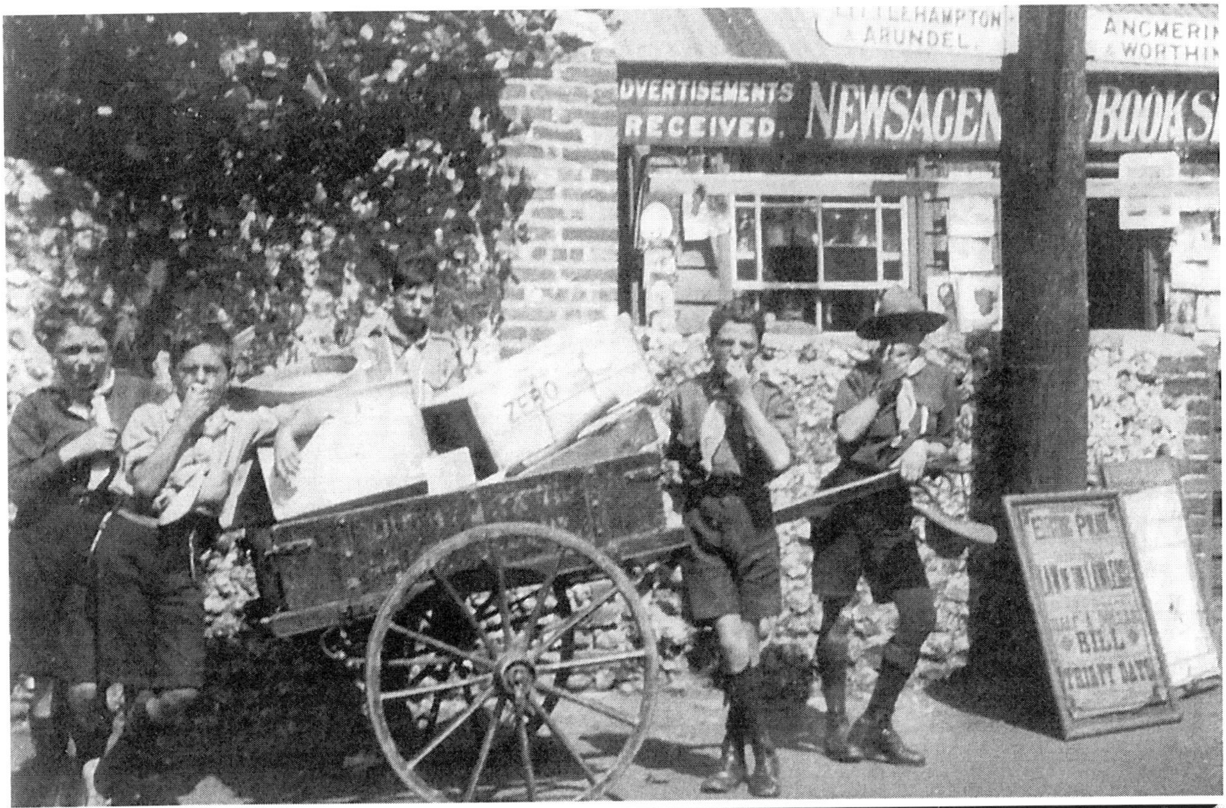
ARUNDEL
DVERTISEMENTS
RECEIVED
NEWSAGEN
ZERO

EHL

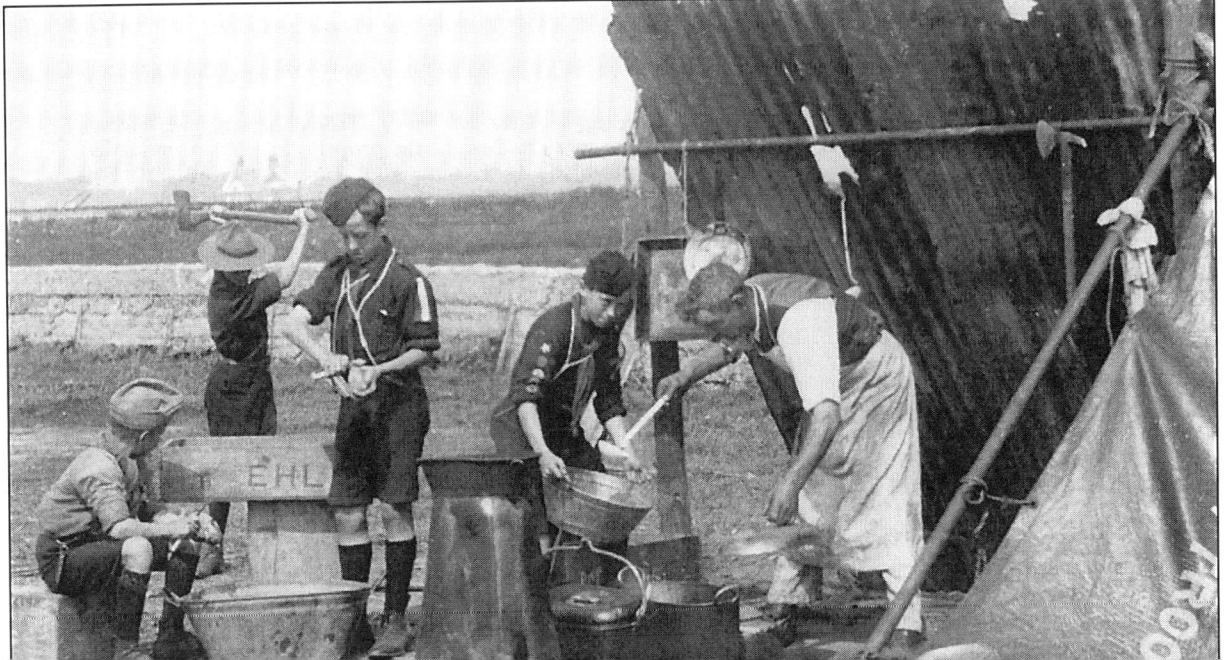

ont. It
ainger
lished

125 Xylophone House, built in 1937 and then called Clist St Mary. Teddy Brown, the famous American xylophonist, renamed it Xylophone House when he bought the property in 1940. Two further owners are recorded, who also changed its name, firstly to Hemmington House and lastly to Bon Accord. In 1976 it suffered the fate of so many fine Rustington properties. Marama Gardens now stands on part of this site.

called
mples,
by the
or the

127 Virginia Cottage. The cottage had its own kitchen, sitting room and double bedroom, all fully furnished. Electricity, water and telephone were all connected. After the 1939/45 war it was used as a private residence, the roof having been raised to allow adult access. It was demolished along with Brough House in 1984. The Gilberts now occupy part of this site.

128 *(left)* Seafield Cottage, showing the entrance to Seafield Court in Sea Lane in 1920. The Pantiles is visible in the left background.

129 *(below left)* Seafield Road, 1927. The sign-board reads 'Rustington Tennis Courts — open to non residents — 2 persons 1/6d, 4 persons 2/6d — tickets at the Pavilion Tea Rooms'. The houses and cottages then were mainly used as holiday accommodation.

130 *(below)* Milk cart, 1927. Mr. F.G. Davies stands by his milk float in Seafield Road. The Rustington Dairy in Broadway Mansions.

131 Sir Hubert Parry, the composer, stands with his wife, Lady Maude, outside Knights Croft, his home in Sea Lane *c.*1903. He was possibly Rustington's most famous resident, and lived here between 1880 and 1918.

132 Knights Croft House. Sir Hubert Parry and Lady Maude Parry go for a stroll in the garden. They had two daughters, Dorothea and Gwendoline and Sir Hubert's yacht 'Dolgwandle' was named after them. Knights Croft House was designed by Norman Shaw, and built by Robert Bushby. The decorative tiles in the house were by William de Morgan, the wallpapers by William Morris.

on the common (e.g. South Field Common). In 1780, the land on both sides of Holmes Lane was called Holmes L[...] Furlong, being within the South Field Common.

obbs
hops

rage,
The

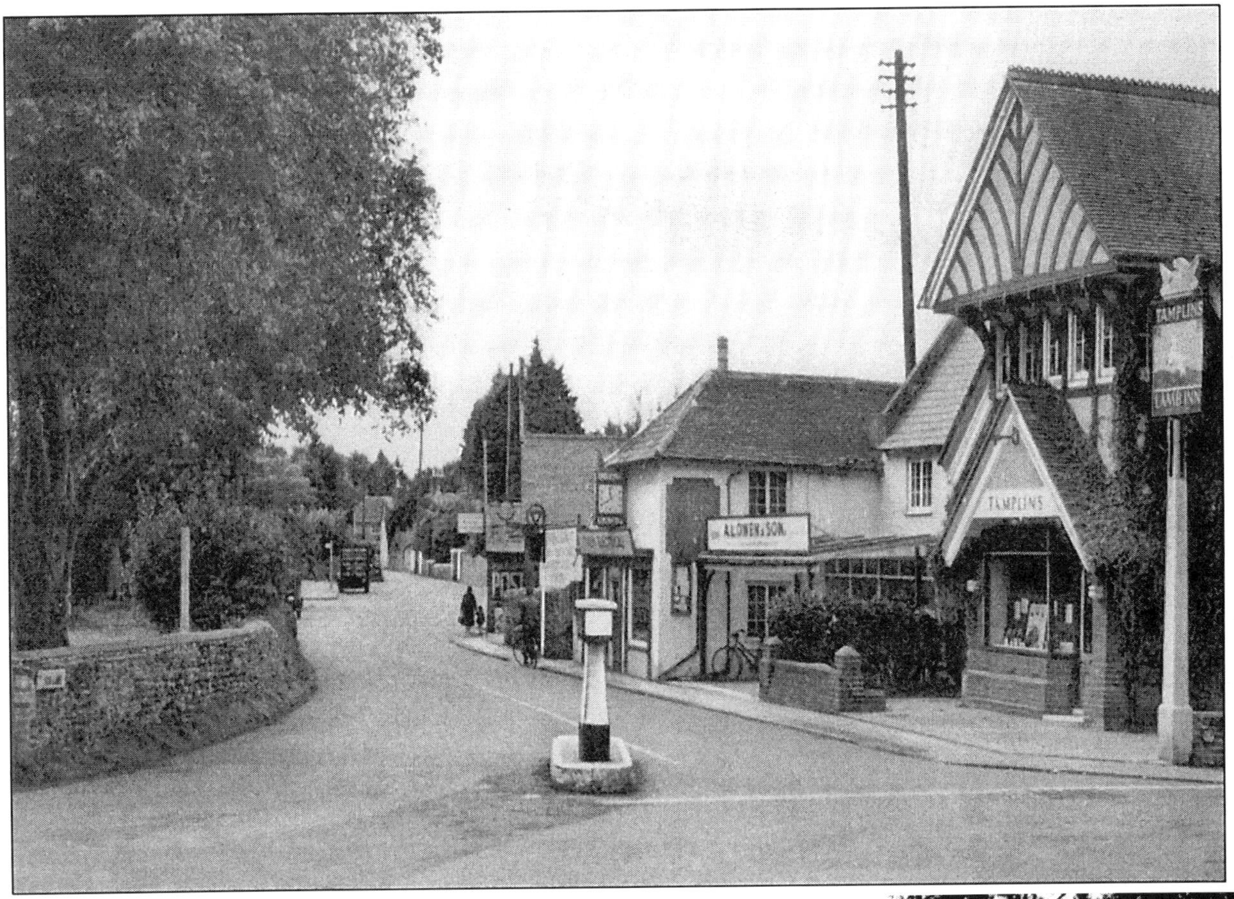

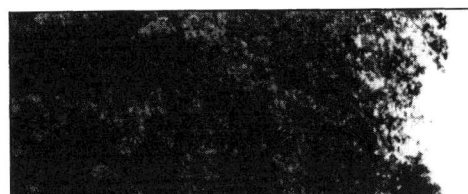

ottage

shop
vaded

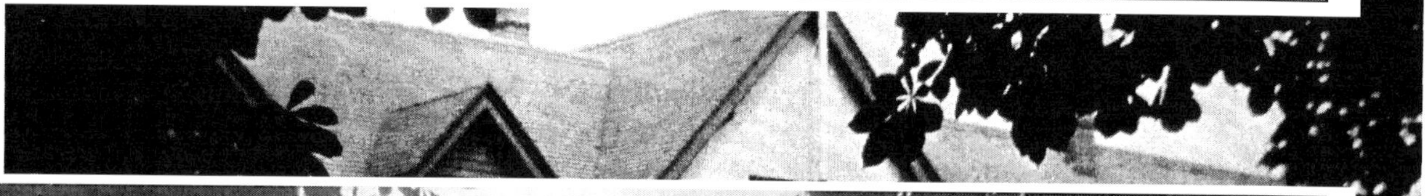

TEL 806
VICTORIA FARM DAIRY

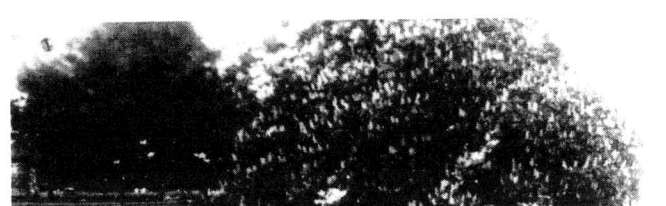

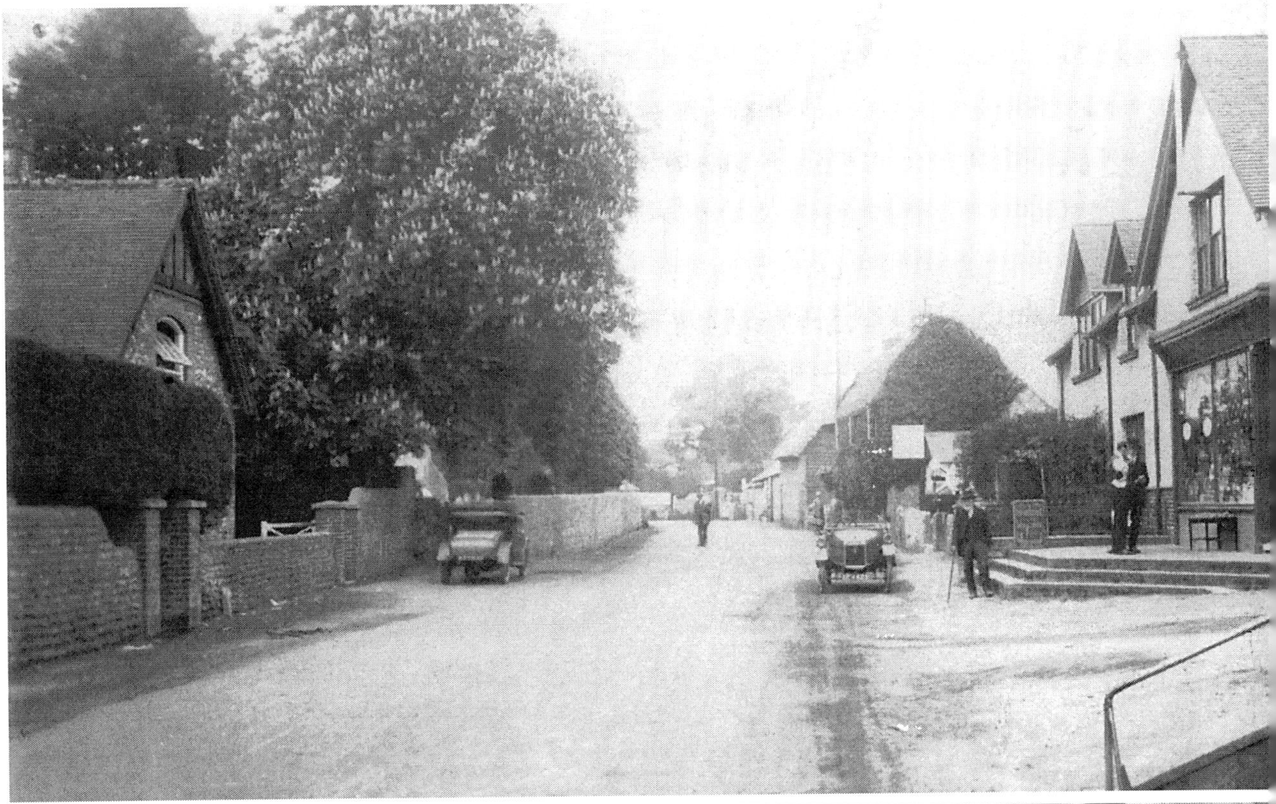

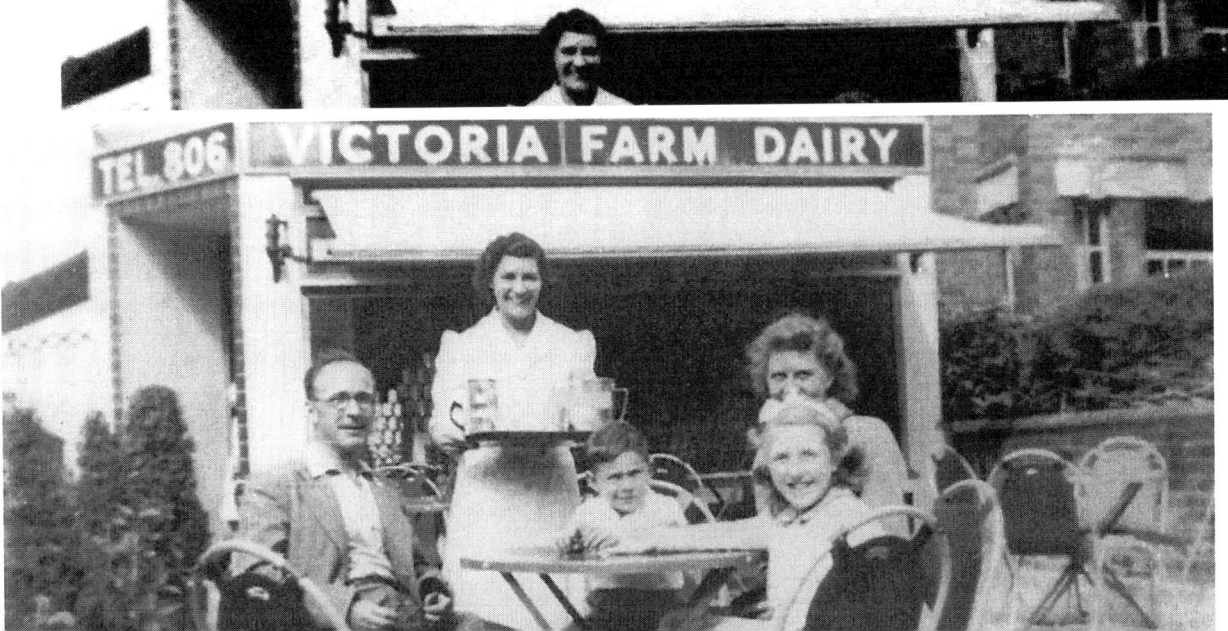

ibout
und',

nged,

146 Broadway Mansions, on the corner of Claigmar Road and The Street, was built by Tom Sum[...] 1909. Many well-known bu[...] were associated with these [...] Ockenden's hardware, Tu[...] chemists, Gladys Brown's woo[...] Yeates greengrocers, Dor[...] butchers, Wingfield The Fisher[...] R. & I. Stacey's to name a fe[...] mansions and flats above[...] demolished in 1973, and replac[...] a building uncharacteris[...] Rustington which now hou[...] controversial Post Office.

147 The Street, *c.*1956, tot[...] unrecognisable today. The N[...] Southdown bus turns round by [...] war memorial in Claigmar R[...] Centre right, elm trees surround C[...] House Fields, where church fêtes [...] garden parties were once held. On [...] left, trees hide Dunnabie/Glentho[...] The Chawtons and The Croft, t[...] residences lost for the developmen[...] the new shops, which now line [...] sides of The Street.

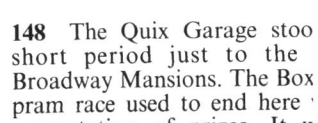

148 The Quix Garage stoo[...] short period just to the [...] Broadway Mansions. The Box[...] pram race used to end here [...] presentation of prizes. It w[...]

149 Dunnabie, built in 1909 as Church House by Mr. Jarrett. Subsequently let and later purchased by the Misses Spalding, who turned it into a guest house. During the 1939/45 war it was requisitioned by troops. After hostilities ceased, the house was purchased by Miss Kathleen Bowler and used as a private school. The house was renamed Glenthorne, and in 1963 it was demolished.

150 The Chawtons was built Humphrey family, and Mrs. Jane Humphrey, the village mistress, lived here. The hou named after the home of auth Austen, who lived in Stev Hampshire, and was demolis 1963.

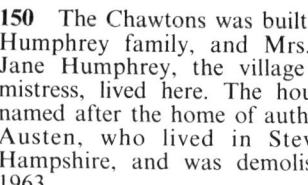

151 The Croft, a lovely double-fronted house, built in The Street during 1896 for Mr. F.C. Chappell, a piano manufacturer. In 1911, Dr. Crosbie Walch, the first resident doctor, came to live here. He was followed by Dr. Ernest Walthen Waller. Surely none of his patients will ever forget him, nor his Victorian waiting-room. This house was also demolished when the Churchill Parade

153 Children in The Street. The Mitchell and L
children, from nearby cottages, pose for photo
Nearby is the footpath that led across the fi
Worthing Road, which was later opened up
Manor Road. Behind the children is Elm Farm

The
uilt

picture

ts for

[t
Ve

f of
use.
her

ard
Miss
Hamilton, Sir Malcolm Fox, and Sir George and Lady Hutchinson. It was requisitioned by the military during the war. Since then Mr. Easter, The Electrical Trades Union (as a convalescent home), Rustington House School and Summerlea School, until its closure in 1986, owned the property. It is now occupied by The Hargreaves Construction Company.

horse.
.1963.

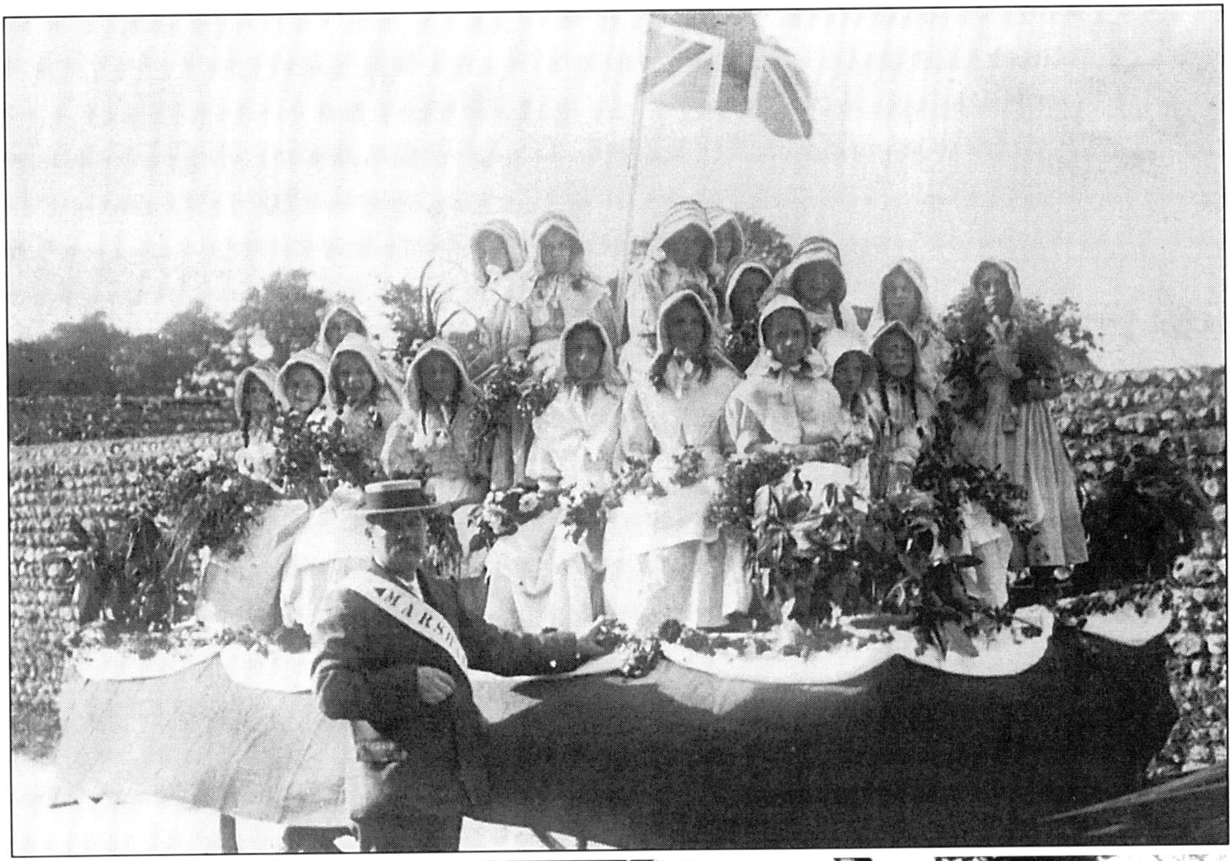

RED CROSS.
HER FIRST PATIENT.

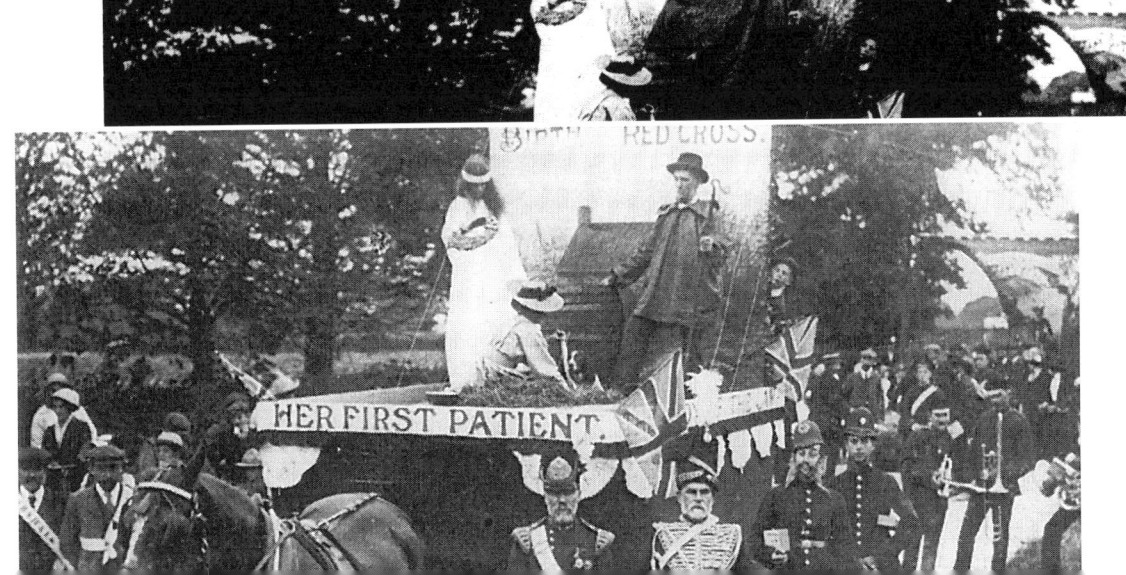

ag at
The

170 *(top right)* Rustington football team in the 1928/29 season, when they were cup winners. Back row (left to right), hon. sec. Mr. Atterbury, Alf Balchin, Les Sopp, A. Bushby, Frank Hoare, Mr. Stoner; Middle row, George Tickner, Sid Atterbury, Cecil Fairs, Eddie Woolven; Front row, Mr. Lane, N. Megenis, George Stanbridge and 'Shirty' Lee.

171 *(right)* Rustington cricket team, *c.*1906. Back row (left to right), Mr. Parmenas Farmener (umpire), Robert Waller, H. Neal, Frank Hoare, Mr. A.H. Shotter, Alan Hoare, Jack MacDonald, Dan Shepherd, Mr. Read; Centre row, James Hoare, Horace Booker, Ernie Sewell, Jack

tions
th a
the
v. J.
h.

173 Coronation Day, 12 May 1937. Police Constable Chappell stands alongside Dr. Waller, who was judging

d for
atron
ner.

ine
ng

tant,
ripp.

177 *(top right)* Elizabethan dancers, led by the coronation carnival princess and her attendants, in the recreation ground, 2 June 1953.

178 *(right)* Members of the Littlehampton bonfire society are introduced to the carnival princess, 2 June 1953. They

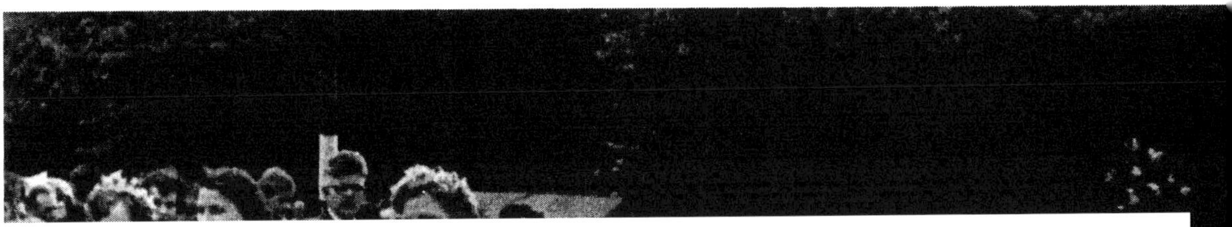

179 *(left)* The square dance float, part of the coronation carnival procession, passing down Sea Lane. George Kilhams is at the wheel of the tractor.

180 *(below left)* The infant welfare float depicted 'The old woman who lived in a shoe'.

181 *(below)* Fancy dress contestants taking part in one of the festivities held on coronation day. Other events were baby shows, Elizabethan, maypole and square dancing displays, sports, a donkey derby, and many side-shows. After a procession around the village, there was dancing for the public, organised by The Rustington Country Dancing Club. Following the Queen's broadcast speech, there was more dancing, this time to the Rustington Square Dance Club. A torch-light procession, starting at 10.30 p.m., ended proceedings for the day.

ation
many

Index

Roman numerals refer to pages in the introduction, and arabic numerals to individual illustratio